BOOK in a BOOK

By: Pauline Roberts

Illustrated by Dasgupta & Soni

McPubKids
www.McPubKids.com

Book in a Book by Pauline Roberts Copyright © 2022 - McPubKids a division of McClure Publishing, Inc.

Published in the United States All Rights Reserved by McClure Publishing, Inc., Bloomingdale, IL 800.659.4908 https://McClurePublishing.com and https://McPubKids.com

Illustrated by Steve Dasgupta and Mayur Soni

Editor: Kathy McClure
Books@McPubKids.com

ISBN: 979-8-9853967-5-1

Printed in the United States

McClure Publishing, Inc.
Bloomingdale, Illinois 60108
Books@McClurePublishing.com

Dedication

This book is dedicated to children who use their imagination

to see art in human form.

I am **BOOK**

Papa Bear reads Book to Baby Bear.

Suddenly, Baby Bear
grabs **Book**!

Baby Bear loves me,
Book thinks.

Baby Bear
crushes
Book!

"Not funny!" **Book** pouts.

"Ouch!" **Book** flinches.

Papa Bear tries to rescue Book.

"I am afraid," Book mumbles.

Baby Bear yanks

Book!

Are we free?
Book's pages wonder.

Book's pages are loose.

Papa Bear says, "The book is ruined."

He tosses Book
into the trash.

"Nooooo!"
Book cries.

Papa Bear calls for Catherine, Baby Bear's sitter to come over.

Catherine watches Baby Bear crawl.

Baby Bear pulls over the trash bin.

Book and trash spill onto the floor.
She picks Book up.

She
opens **Book's**
covers.

Book's
pages fall.

Catherine gasps!

She throws Book back into the trash.

"Um!"
Book frowns.

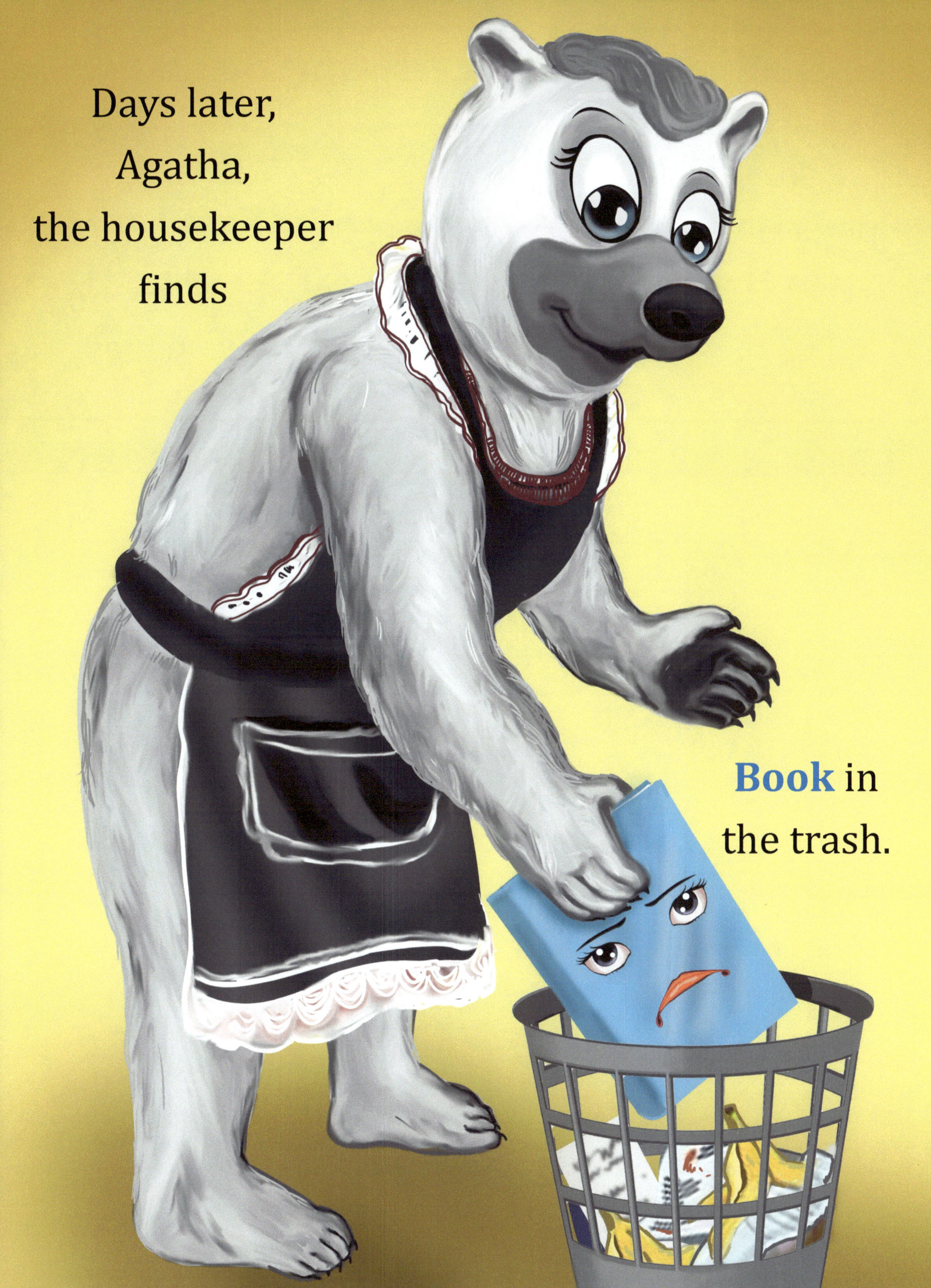
Days later,
Agatha,
the housekeeper
finds

Book in
the trash.

She
opens Book's
covers.

She
sees no
pages.

"I need
help!"
Book
whimpers.

Agatha
searches the
trash for

Book's pages.

She takes **Book** home

and saves Book from the stinky garbage truck.

Agatha tries to restore **Book** for her Baby Bear.

She glues
its pages.

"It tickles!"
Book
wiggles.

She blows on **Book** to dry
the pages.

"It's nippy!"
Book shivers.

She irons to smooth out the wrinkles.

"Its scary!"
Book
screams.

With just a
glimpse of the
steam puffer,

the wrinkles
runaway.

It takes a while to fix
Book's smile.

Thanks
to Agatha, I am
back on the shelf
again.
Book sighs.

Book is happy
to be with new
friends,

but
its more excited
to see the new
Baby Bear,

and Book is eager
to play.

Book longs for the good old days, good times and starts to daydream of a wonderful life with the new Baby Bear.
Lots of chuckles,
endless giggles,
deep belly laughs,

and the many funny faces when Baby Bear flip
my pages.

Baby Bear clings to **Book**.

Everywhere Baby Bear goes,
Book goes too!

In the car,

to the park,

to see the doctor, and

to bed.

"Baby Bear is my best friend,

and

I am Baby Bear's favorite

Storybook!"

says **Book**.

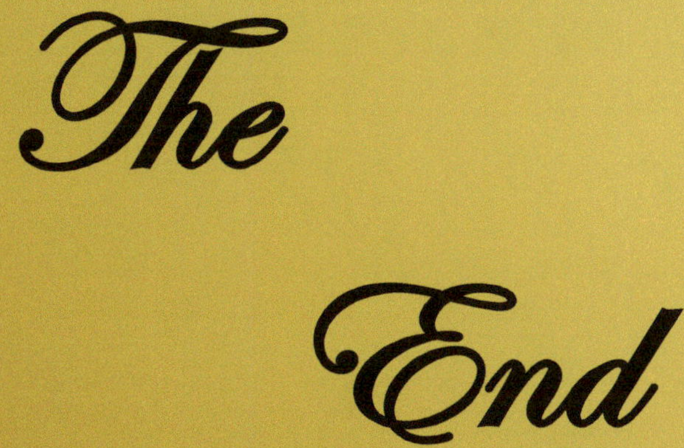

The

End